The Multitude

The Multitude

Hannah Faith Notess

Co-winner of the 2014 Michael Waters Poetry Prize

Published by the University of Southern Indiana
Evansville, Indiana

ISBN 978-1-930508-33-0   First Edition

Printed in the USA

Library of Congress Control Number: 2015949080

Southern Indiana Review Press
Orr Center #2009
University of Southern Indiana
8600 University Boulevard
Evansville, Indiana 47712

sir.press@usi.edu
usi.edu/sir
Ron Mitchell & Marcus Wicker, eds.

Cover art: *Flowering Fossil Bed* by Gala Bent; *galabent.com*

Cover design: BeckyJo Bourgeois & Zach Weigand

For Jon

Contents

III

◆

Endor (Disambiguation)

In a hut in the Star Wars universe,
on the forest moon of Endor,
a creature carefully draws a map
of things connected to other things.

The creature draws a road between
two worlds, because one Elvish name
for Tolkien's Middle-earth is also
this forest moon or the planet
the forest moon orbits—
on this point the Star Wars universe is unclear.

Maybe our universe has a finite number
of times you can summon the dead
so we've begun to repeat ourselves.

Endor, ancient Canaanite village,
home of the witch who conjured Samuel.
Endor, Palestinian village,
depopulated. Endor, Israeli kibbutz.
Endor, the most successful town
in *Dragon Quest IV: Chapters of the Chosen*.

So who can blame the Israelite king
for wanting his best prophet
back from the land of the dead?

Who can blame the witch,
who only did what was asked of her?
Endor, forest moon, home place.

There were so many worlds
I longed to visit as a child,
where the creatures, the citizens,
would line up along the street
to say, *Welcome friend, welcome stranger.*

I

Burlington Northern Apocalypse

Burlington, Washington

It's that time of night, pilgrim, you know
the one I mean, when heartache wails through town
and all the dogs and ghosts sit up
then lie back down, sighing, *no, not this time.*

It wakes you like the call to prayer you first heard
years ago, unfurled from half-a-dozen minarets
in a blue city, and when those voices shook the floor,
you heard quite plainly, *God is great,*

what are you doing here? So you came home, rode
line after creaking line until some boxcar
dumped you in this cloud-swamped scrap of a town
swept so clean by God's broom

all that's left is a shuttered hardware store
and the diminished chord that rides the Doppler down
then slinks away to die in a rusted-out railyard.
If, in this moment, you can still believe

the voice that rouses you is still the voice
that called you back from somewhere east
to these souls you left for dead years ago,
then follow this: a single line for your single

mind, a prayer that rumbles north-northwest,
past dead boxcars, the graveyard, flooded fields,
dikes, migrant camps, moss-ruined barracks, past
land stuttering into marsh and island, past coast

after coast until the curtain of mist rises
and all that's left is water, air, and whatever's
out there—admit you don't know, admit it—
dark, plain, quiet, bottomless, and cold.

To the Body Carried Out of the Apartment Across the Street

Sometimes I pretend I don't live anywhere
real, at least not here, the Ballard–Interbay Industrial Area
a dented sign welcomes us to. You must have
tried this, too: closing your eyes, making the incessant hum
of cars on pavement sound like waves on the beach,
the way when you're a kid your mother tells you
to hold the shell to your ear to hear the ocean.

After they rolled you out in the blank zipped-up bag
and the medical examiner's van pulled away,
traffic stopped slowing down. I went indoors,
and so did the neighbors, divorced dad and ex-frat boy.
Whatever happened to you, it worked.

But you should know: the sun rises earlier and earlier now.
The crocuses next to the dumpster are opening
their fat purple mouths. The mail continues to arrive
on time; the recycling is still emptied every Thursday,
and when the glass bottles shatter, I plug my ears
and wonder what sound could wake you, and what color
is the blankness that your blank eyes see.

Street Fighter II for a Broken Sega Genesis

Our hands remember the feint and jab
but nothing works the way it used to.

Brought forth from tangled wires—the battles
we thought we'd abandoned, sloughed off as we grew,

but couldn't bear to throw away.
So there they are, in the 10-foot storage unit,

in the back aisle at the Goodwill, in a yard sale bin,
or in the same air-conditioned basements where we spent

all summer in combat to what circular purpose—to defeat
each other in endless knockout rounds.

So the heat comes back to our blood.
Most of the buttons do nothing, but you've found

a way to swipe my feet from under me—
your lone trick move, no matter what guise

you assume. Bodies remember: blow on the cartridge;
bang on the console when the picture freezes.

And though I jump in one direction only,
no longer master of the lightning kick, simplicity

makes our quarrel beautiful. My adversary, my beloved,
fight me, fight on with your one good claw.

Chess by Mail

I write this for you, who will never read it.
You're standing at a window
overlooking a lower level of the afterlife,
rows of card catalogs and microfiche machines,
academic journals with spines uncracked—
the memory apparatus we don't use
anymore. Do you remember the game
we played in another life? The life of aerograms
and twenty-five-cent stamps, when index cards
held gambits, codes, verses, binomials.
You let me rearrange the pieces,
not by how they're meant to move
because (you said) the queen
moves any direction. I am not the queen.
I do not move any direction
but west, but forward in time
to your library as you left it, the weighted pieces
high on their shelf. In this life,
your commonplace books line bottom shelves,
pasted with postcards, poems, editorials, old news.
If I reassembled them would it re-
assemble you? No? Pawn to queen four.

The Disaster Tourist

I was three hundred miles north
on the beach when the tsunami hit.

It foamed up gently around my belly,
soaking my towel and the pages
of a ratty paperback.

◆

When the boy's body came to the hospital,
plucked like a rag off the barbed wire,

I sat downstairs in the front office
wrestling with the ancient Dictaphone.
Its heavy pedal kept rewinding
to a blank stretch of tape.

◆

The morning the hurricane swallowed a city,
a bus careened around the corner
in a wave of rain, drenching my new clothes.

I arrived angry and wet, complained
to the girl, who, eight months later,
would misjudge her landing in the fog,

transfiguring her small plane
into a ball of flame.

◆

To the stupid angel of death, I want to say,
you missed me again!

Watch me disappear into the train depot,
into the past, just before the bombing.

Watch me lean awkwardly against
the flashing height-weight-horoscope machine,
clutching my shabby luggage in the spot

you could have caught me, if the taxi driver
had taken four months to arrive.

Under the Curse

Sometimes the girl with a toad for a heart
forgets. Whole hours, it just blinks at the world
from between her ribs, and even beats,
heartlike, till it grows scared or hungry.

And when the fox-headed architect
walks to work on a sunny morning,
he gazes up into glass towers, where furred
shadows scurry through the vacant condos—
and lets himself think that he's not alone.

Sometimes the placebo works.
In the winter sun, the singer
with knives for bones sits quilt-wrapped,
holding her dozing husband's hand.

His narcoleptic snoring sounds
like old music. And though his brain lies
buried far away in snow, he dreams of birdsong
and budding branches, credulous.
Sometimes the crown of the horned baby's head

just slides into the world. Sometimes
the blighted tree bears fruit.
And as for the stone-eyed grandmother
who threw her glasses out to pray for healing,

even she, in her long insomniac
Bible-reading nights, will come
to a story she knows, just close
her glossy eyes, keep reading,
and forget that she can't see the words.

To the Former Self in Art Class

You didn't know the boy who sat next to you
in Watercolor 101 was going to shut himself
in his car, stop breathing. Let's be honest.
His cones and cylinders were as lopsided
as everyone else's cones and cylinders.

When you hear the news two years later,
you search your own tatty portfolio
for clues and sigh, *If only I had known*—
but I want to shake you and say, *You didn't*,
and anyway that phrase is a stupider knife

even than Occam's old razor. If you went back,
with your gray lens of knowledge, you'd still be painting
the same burnt-out cathedral under burnt-orange
blood dripping from the sky, collaged with quotations
from *The Waste Land*. You thought it meant

you were losing your faith; but look, there you are
sitting in church, five years in the future,
and wondering (like a good Protestant) why
you want so much to pray for the souls of the dead.
In fact, you could go back and forth enough

times to wear a rut in the floor of time,
but your awkward brushstrokes would still paint
a cathedral that lists to the left. You'd still
stay up all night worrying about the alchemical
substance of the soul. Your grand attempts

at phthalo yellow sunrises would still turn murky,
while the same boy sat silent beside you,
washing the globe of an apple with quinacridone
gold, shading it with Payne's gray,
the same damp worm asleep on his heart.

Anatevka, Indiana

There's no use in it now, ancestor—weeping
along the old country's riverbank,
where the farm-fouled water rises
imperceptibly each year. No one

remembers you except drunk farmhands
sprawled in the rushes, daring each other
to chase your reedlike white legs
in moonlight. You wish you'd

boarded a steamer years ago.
Bind up your dripping hair. Put on your shoes,
kiss every doorframe of the unreal shtetl
if you must. It's time to haunt

a new country; our chemical-burned fields
are ripe for ghosts. Come walk the peeled-paint
streets of our small town; we'll welcome you home
to your own ghostlight above the stage

where every weekend night the high school
chorus mourns you, where, after curtain calls,
an understudy lingers among the setpieces,
tracing square letters with her fingers.

The Witch and the Soldier

Every time I bring a boy back from the dead
to make love to, something goes wrong.

At first I conjured only torsos,
and until the third year of the war
nearly all arrived armless.

This boy appears at the window
dressed only in a towel,
which ribbons into a million-mile sheet
as soon as I unwind it.

How is the war, Darling? I ask. He says,
We never die how we're supposed to.

It takes us years to undress; his marble arms
fumble through mountains of cold cloth.
I am wearing a green sari that flows

into the next room, its pleats unpinnable.
The young ones, they mostly just want to stay dead.
And when at last he comes to me,

his touch is shards of glass; drops
of ghost water bead on his skin,
and ice the air
into sprays of chandeliers

but who wants to make love on a bed of chandeliers?
He doesn't mind; he has
so little left, except for me.

Philippians

I used to forget my Greek New Testament on purpose,
so the future seminarians would share with me.
They smelled like sweat and prayer
and oatmeal cookies, and trying too hard
to get God to love them, too hard.

In a notebook carried back
from Africa, just to be different,
I copied out the Greek
in my best handwriting.
Rejoice, rejoice, we translated,
but I didn't want to; instead
I skulked around campus, brooding
about why God wasn't born a woman.

The seminarians were growing their beards
in a very apostolic style.
One of them was headed to India that summer
to get dirty for Jesus, while another
used to sit outside the chapel for hours,
arm around his small, weeping girlfriend.
It must have been a difficult life.

Now the building where
we used to push our desks into a circle
has burned to the ground.

Rejoice, rejoice, the book kept saying,
and Jesus kept getting jerked
between heaven and earth
like a jumping jack on a string
called *kenosis,* emptying
and filling himself again.
At that time, Saint Paul
was imprisoned in another country.

By now the seminarians have taken up
youth groups and wives and children.
Or they became the gawky white giant
in the photograph of smiling brown orphans.

I don't know why
some buildings burned to cinders
instantly, while others
only turned a little gray,
just kissed by ash and smoke,
and I don't know why
God touches down on some of us
and not on others,

and I don't know why sometimes
a prisoner doesn't even have
a window to look out of
when he writes, *Rejoice, rejoice*,
and other times
an earthquake rattles him free.

A Guide for Spiritual Tourists

It told us whether to cover our heads,
where to remove our sandals.
It told us not to wear shorts if male
and if female to be careful.

It said *Speak slowly please. That's too expensive.*
Drive slowly. Stop here. Please call a doctor.
It said to tip the man guarding the shoes.

He lined our sandals neatly on the steps
facing the dark-mouthed dome.
We approached barefoot, our feet damp
as someone swept water with a stiff broom.

It said *Excuse me. I don't understand.*
I'm lost. I'm pregnant. I've been robbed. I want
to get off. I need a larger room.

Inside, rows of sandstone saints
with extra eyes. Or a black-tongued woman.
Or Francis Xavier's remains.
Or a rosy square with pigeons and a bath.
Or a cupboard of scrolls. Or a gilded man,
cross-legged or on a cross. Or tree limbs
coiled with flags. But always incense,
worn pavement, smoke-stained walls.

It said *Where are you going? Is this it,*
the train for Calcutta? May I have
a kilo of mangoes? How much is it?
Where are my shoes? Please help me.

We left just as we entered, blinking
our cameras at the courtyard,
holding these small pronouncements in our hands.

In the City of Arias

I believe it is a little like the place
        we go each night before we airdrop into sleep,

that there, the girls in uncomfortable shoes
        kick them off in the deep grass
                stepping off sidewalks, off stages,

and the woman in the elaborate witch wig
        has unpinned her heavy tresses,
                now free to walk bald in the street.

The lover, freed of his costume sword
        and rage-filled alto girlfriend
no longer has to sing that vengeance
        is kind of like justice.

Actual songs perch in the trees—
the words are untranslatable.

In that city, I want to say,
        the voice is the lamp of the body,

and if a soprano falls accidentally
        from her rooftop garden
she will release only one clear note,
        its pitch diving Doppler away from you.

I want to believe you have moved
        into a building of bel canto vowels,

that your voice,
        clear as an empty room,
                has an apartment all to itself.

There, I believe, every steel beam carries one note
        and every brick rests on others to form a chord,
                and even a crumpled airplane

flares open like a fermata nearly resolved.
In that city, anyone can endure it.

St. Augustine Enters the World's Largest Pac-Man Maze

What is the soul, my God,
but a point of light
propelled by desire?
I was born in darkness.
Through rooms and corridors,
through palaces of memory,
through stadia and fora,
I seek you, my Creator,
yet pursued by heresies
and ghosts of heresies.
Carthage, Rome, Milan,
Hippo—one forum looks
much like another.
What does the cornered
soul devour? What fruit
revives it? How does
it slip through death,
split open, wilt, then
dissolve into the very
fabric of the world? Enlarge me
thus. As water flows the same
through every city's aqueducts,
so let me pass through
these worlds. Oh, I will search
every corner of each city.
I will stand at the edge
of this empire and pray
into the dark, yet
will I hunger.

To the Girl Playing Mario Kart in the Botticelli Room

Uffizi Gallery, Florence, Italy

Oh really? There's nothing more fascinating in this life
    than a jumpy little mushroom
        bobbing along in a go-kart? Here we are, slumped
in front of masterpieces, the tour guide nattering
    distinguished names and dates through our earbuds.
        Meanwhile Toadstool careens down palm-lined avenues,
edging Yoshi off-track for the win.
    Die, baby dinosaur, die! Who has time
        to genuflect before the skeletons
whose brushes once stroked innumerable dressfolds?
    Let them rest in their recycled sarcophagi.
        Now I know, this being a poem, I am supposed
to come out flags flying for the Old Masters.
    For savoring the polished skin
        of the fruit-breasted Madonna also known as Venus.
For soothing your exhausted dad
    who thought you could use a little culture.
        Against your twitchy thumbs and shriveled brain.
But why should I? You're content
    in this sweltering room that just happens to be adorned
        with the elaborate bequests of bloodthirsty jerks,
who'd totally have torched you if you looked
    at them wrong. And the Graces who sway through
        Spring don't give a crap, absorbed in their game
of "Who can step on the most flowers?"
    Art ignores us. Fast-forward fifty years
        and there's a Galleria Shigeru Miyamoto
where 8-bit clouds scroll serenely by
    above the corner where your leggy granddaughter
        is crouched with some unnamed device
inventing her own masterpiece—an antiquated city
    of ladies slouched in elevated walkways
        fanning themselves and peering down at the butchers,

the tanners, the cart drivers, at the models
        on their way to the studio, where they'll stand
               in their underwear for hours, fingers intertwined,
while the gray-eyed apprentice shuffles draperies
        around them. His warm fingers,
              their cool shoulders. Not a bad life, this.

Haight Street, Halloween

Over and over, the air blazed,
incinerated

itself. We were not yet in love. I turned
to a shop window

crammed with snaky fuschia wigs and acid-trip
posters, but watched

your face flicker, grayed to an etching
in the plate glass.

I caught the light on your chin,
hardly noticed

we waded waist high in little witches
and turtles.

A pumpkin gaped up at my face,
then loped along

in search of candy. The teacher who brought up
the line flapped by

silently, a giant mother bat in striped socks.
How many times

has the thing I wanted stayed hidden from me,
obscured by my longing?

Turn, oh, turn to me, I said, without
opening my mouth.

On the Drill Field at Virginia Tech

The boy, age four, stands at the edge,
        pressed up against the chain-link fence.

He can just reach between the wire squares
        to touch the still-damp grass.
            He's listening.

His head swivels; he hears each snare beat
        ricochet in air, off warm stone buildings,

four staggered tones of tuned bass drums
        and quads, rising in cadences
            you still can't quite locate.

And yes, you're there
        beside your brother, you're
            age six and anxious, rattling the fence

since you're too short to see.
        But then it rises, the glittering edge
            of the band, a distant mass of white

uniforms. You might see it then—the sound
        you can't quite hear, translated into light,
            the sound that makes him remember

a moment you'll mostly forget—
        a band in constant motion,
            the folding lacework

of waves at the sea's edge,
        rising, receding, figures
            and instruments flashing,

the sun so bright
        there is no color
                but this field, the green

swath of it marked
        by nothing but the lines
                of longing etched

in white across it,
        from child to sound
                and sound and sound—

What happens next is easier:

The boy grows up to become a bandleader.

You grow up to learn to read music
        then forget it.

The field grows up to become a crime scene.

Pages crawl with black beetle notes.

And what now is scrawled on the green page
        at the bottom of your brain?

The band does not grow up,
        but persists—a constant
                waving, folding thing;

squares shift into lines and back—
        You should be far enough away now
                to perceive this. But you misremembered—

there is no fence at all. This field
        is open to anyone, webbed by white paths,
                altogether absent of uniforms and children.

You plot a point at the listening boy,
        then draw a line through time
                to where you sit remembering this,

like all those lines
        carved through the grass
                could map the future for you

like you still have a chance to hear it,
to be caught up in that wave of sound.

A Natural History

An expert from the First Baptist Church
in coat and tie came with our class to the Nature
and Science Museum, to lead the second grade
past the error-filled placards on the walls
of the Prehistoric Hall, so we could
admire in innocence the skeletons
of God's magnificent extinct Creation.

I hung back as the class clambered through
the echoing hallway of the woolly mammoth.
I picked out vowels in the word *pro-to*
ZO-a, almost pronounced *eu-KAR-y-ote*
before the teacher grabbed my hand and pulled
me back to where the expert stood beside
a fossil of perplexing mollusks, which,
though lovely, he allowed, was still wrong.
How boring evolution seemed; how long
its squiggly creatures took to surface
from brown pools onto the muddy bank,

while back at Christian school the brontosauri
galumphed through Eden, upending flocks
of peacocks and passenger pigeons, still sleepy-eyed
and newborn. Pterodactyls perched atop
the tree of life, while lazy mammoths swung
their heavy tusks, thumping small mammals
left and right, not killing them, just bruising
because (the expert said) there was no death
before man's fall, except for vegetables.

I want to be a scientist when I
grow up! I wrote and drew a hundred stick-
legged birds, colored each with a different crayon.
I didn't yet know to hope for Darwin's
jewel-eyed finches, fluttering in the back pages
of the story, each variegated beak
singing its slightly mutated note.

The Witch and the Scientist

In the damp hoophouses
we fell down together, between green rows
(labeled by chromosome)
of sweet, spice-scented leaves,
and when I shuddered,
he said, *earthquake*, and kissed my thighs, my knees.

We worked the same
way. Strand by strand, we teased
the world apart
and twisted it together, shaping
with knot and helix
and spiderweb, the newest breathing thing.

I thought he'd understand
when I lit up the moon's dark side
for him at sunset.
Instead, he drew me nearer
and whispered, *earthshine*,
sunlight reflected by our atmosphere.

And when I stormed,
he said, *cloudburst.* And when I cursed him,
he was stricken,
and he buried the mutation deep in his brain,
vowing one day
to conjure a body free of pain.

Mario World

After the layoff, enemies multiplied
like ghosts. For days we wandered, hands grown cold,
eyes glazed, blood slowed. You showed me how to hold
it together. We slid across sheets of ice,
bounded down hills, but met so much disaster
I despaired. *You don't need to kill them all,*
you said, pulling me up the castle wall
past missed jumps, wasted lives, buried treasure.
Brother, so many times I died not believing
it teaches you to play it as you play.
But I'm learning. We can't catalogue each
killer we'll meet or guess which creatures hatch
a new world for us. Ghosts find us every day,
but we'll go back to gather what we need.

To the Ghost Who Put His Arm Around Me at the Camp Meeting

Cane Ridge, Kentucky

who made the spirit sound easier
than falling in love, to whom I said,
Tell me about this holiness,
and make me some room
on the anxious bench,
if you can. To the ghost
with long eyelashes beaded
with the baptizing water,
to the ghost with the fiery voice:
Dear boy, I won't repudiate you.
But you are all prayer and wind.
Tongues of flame. I remind you
of your own flesh, the cat
skulking and turning in the grave.
My pleated skirts billow and furl
like the tent above us.
Unknot my bonnet. When I lean
into your heartbeat, I hear spoons knocking,
the plucked fiddle and jug.

Yoshi (A Pastoral)

Meet me in arcadia
the forest where I was born
under trees taller
than you can believe
and believe their invisible boughs
map the world for us
and believe their fruit
will sustain us forever
We'll leap from branch to branch
like warriors who sail
through bamboo stalks
still earthbound but lightly
and I will devour everything
that wants to harm you
Even the deserts will bloom
with brilliant sand blossoms
and the mountain slopes will glitter
snow-clad through summer
And though I cannot consume
your ghosts or enter the ruined
palaces of your memory
beloved I will wait for you
always in the roadless shade
as proof of my devotion
Dearest friend return
to the place we first met
and I will be reborn
and reborn and reborn

Compliment

You said my naked back looked strong to you.
My sloped, hunched shoulders flickered in my brain,
but then I thought of the junior high girl
I briefly became—who cut the pictures out
of her ballet books, who rewound the tape
of Fonteyn draping her back like silk across
Nureyev's arm, then turned her own small back
to the bathroom mirror. Every variation
of that shape she could think of, she practiced,
till her muscles tensed like twisted swing chains
on the playground. Unwound, stretched to her limit,
she pushed against the future and reached me,
her future. I arched my back, a bridge to her,
and said, half to her, half to you, *Thank you.*

Pallas Athena

Standing before my father's bookcase,
I pretended I had sprung from his head
able to read it all—Hesse, Norse
sagas, my great-great-grandfather's

Russian apothecary texts.
The shelf below these five browned
volumes (now bound in wood-print
contact paper) held the same man's

chess set. They said he often
confused the king and queen, since
Russian men were short and fat,
their women tall and queenly.

I wanted to be the girl who skipped
everything girlish, to be born
gray-eyed and clear-skinned, to yell
with the raspy voice of a boy.

In this dream, I was moving troops
and surly heroes from square to square
of my gameboard Greece. They besieged
the best cities. My face floated above

the place philosophers came to die.
They brought me wreaths and metered hymns.
Later, I learned the Parthenon
was once painted, gaudy golds and reds

daubed its famous frieze. Then I learned
parthenos was virgin, feminine noun
with a masculine ending.
In the temple's center a squat idol

fed on the prayers of frightened soldiers.
Now I know its pillars bow, an optical illusion
framing the square womb where all day
tourists wander in and around.

Part of the Problem with the Witch

The ovens themselves were not so frightening;
they were not the convection-heated
wonder the witch wanted, just metal
trash cans, their insides coated in clay.

The villagers baked their bread
by wrapping dough around hot stones,
dropping them in, then stoking the coals.
What frightened us? Her sighs,

her constant calling of our names,
the scrape of her fingernails
as she ran her hands over and over our heads.
Nights, she kept me up while my brother slept,

telling me how her father—a con man,
a trance-faking sage—had run off with the woman
who sold him his snake-charming snakes.
What could I say to that? She waited out my silence;

we heard my brother sighing in his dreams,
the house turning shakily on its chicken legs.
Which reminds me, the ovens were not
even hers, just something we saw the day

she took us out to the bazaar, holding
one of us tightly in each hand.
Look there—she gripped our fingers—*in this country
they eat breaded stone. Aren't you amazed?*

Your Own Calcutta

"Stay where you are. Find your own Calcutta."

—Mother Teresa

My Calcutta browses the brown bookshop on Mirza Ghalib Road.
He opens a book to the map of his Calcutta, because inside
my Calcutta is a miniature Calcutta I don't know how to navigate.

Someone's Calcutta rides the silent underground back and forth
in the darkness. Her Calcutta clutches luggage
in the back seat of an Ambassador barreling down Bose Road

like a shark. I am my Calcutta's and he is mine. Your Calcutta
is nearly a boy, running the Calcutta Sound and Light Show
for the Nth night in a row. His schoolgirl Calcutta perches on the bars

of her brother's bicycle. Her Calcutta, in the Maidan, has just bowled
in an interminable cricket game, because for her Calcutta,
Sunday never ends. In the Barabazaar, one Calcutta holds up her arms

to be measured for a blouse. Our Calcutta is a city of the mind,
now spelled Kolkata. The women decorate Mother Teresa's tomb
with marigolds because it is white and bare. You travelled to Calcutta

all the way from Argentina to carry this sopping basket of Calcutta laundry
to this roof, where, hanging sheets, you can see to the Howrah Bridge.
Our Calcuttas stacked one on another could reach the moon.

To the Witch Who Gave My Sister Knives for Bones

Your bad temper stank up the room at once
when you entered, hanging on you like

your rolls of fat, or was it your sadness,
draped over your shoulders like a ratty shawl?

Bright moth bodies fluttered in your stringy hair.
When you told us that the curse had taken

even though the child wasn't screaming yet,
you wiped your scabby hands on your apron,

and waddled away, hunched under the cloud
of invective we sent after you out the door.

I watched you climb into the oxcart
and settle your bulk next to the brute-faced devil

who spat on you and flicked his whip
to drive you, curse by curse, village by village

further from your mountain home, each day
another blade to sharpen on your fingernails,

each day closer to the stinking city, all blinking neon
legs, black eyes, razor blades, where—you must

have been thinking—there were enough sick kids
already, where you would finally be free.

Ghost House Level

Think of all the farthest places you reached
in all the video games you never finished.
Think of the tunnels down, the spiral staircase
into hell. Think of your hand along the worn
wood banister, of gripping the gamepad
till the buttons blistered your thumbs. Think of
the monsters in the corners of the maps
you made. Think of the scores you settled,
scores you saved. Think of the ghosts you made
to race against, faint doppelgängers driving
just ahead of you, diving off-track into darkness.
You played so long you lost all thought of an ending
and took up your residence among the shades.
Think of the empty rooms, the doors kicked open.
Think of the woman weeping on the stairs.
When you go in, no one can go with you.
Parts of you are still there waiting for you.

To the Church Across the Bridge Who is Claiming the City for God

Greetings. I lost track of the souls I was supposed to save.
The barges dredge and dredge, but turn up
nothing, and the drawbridge gapes open

like the gulf between Man and God, but nobody
is waiting to cross over, nobody wants to switch sides.

Back in high school I lacked the will to carry tracts,
to save even the skinny Catholic boy
who put his arm around me in computer class;

when we learned the world was made of zeroes
and ones, I could see that scroll unfold, a stack

of perforated sheets, zig-zagging up to heaven,
etched with gray dot-matrix marks
only a nitpicky God would read.

Now, it's a whole city, gorgeous, godless.
It hurts to watch the world split down the middle.

It hurts also to drift into the dark.
So, when your judgment day unspools
like ticker tape from downtown windows

and all the screens go blank, I won't show up
to cheer. I'll wait it out down by the canal,

watching the rowers slide their shells and sculls
between the two peninsulas
that wish to become an isthmus once again.

Meditation on the Divine Blueness
with Two Pop Songs

Rishikesh, India

It's just that in "My Sweet Lord" George Harrison
sounds so *Jesusy*, with his platoon of earnest handclappers
and strummers on backup, transparent

like the Maranatha choruses of my childhood
slapped verse by verse onto the overhead projector.
And so I start to think it's really still 1968 here.

I got the song's joke the first time, but here
I hear it for myself—in the Rishikesh German Indian
Chinese Israeli Continental Bakery—*Hare Krishna*

is just two syllables away from *Hallelujah*
and "My Sweet Lord" is not even two notes away
from "He's So Fine" (*doo lang doo lang doo lang*)

and Jesus is just two notes away from Krishna
but in flesh-colored makeup, too shy to show us
his true blue skin. It's 1968, and the Beatles

are decked in saffron garlands,
posing in a row around the Maharishi,
this gleaming green river behind them,

under a god's-skin blue February sky. It's 1968
and I'm staring at the same green February water, wishing
the Australians upstairs would just

put the damn sitars away. Any minute now
it'll be 1971, and George's new backup singers
will get out their tambourines and start clapping

like some scruffy kids picked up at a beachside revival, squinting
at the transliterated mantras *Rama Rama Hare Hare.*
It's 1971 and—really, I'm not stoned—the Chiffons

are suing George Harrison for royalties
(*doo lang doo lang doo lang*) and incidentally, Krishna
is suing Jesus because he thought of incarnation first.

Jesus swears it was an accident; he didn't mean to copy,
but the court doesn't care. And anyway, it's 1975 now and my dad,
long-haired, is sitting cross-legged in a work shirt

and bell bottoms with a guitar
on somebody's living room floor in Virginia,
strumming the same chords, a mimeographed

scripture song. *I really wanna see you, Lord, but it takes
so long, my Lord.* It's 1975 and the Chiffons are recording
"My Sweet Lord" (*doo lang doo lang doo lang*)

as a joke: the magic's over. We missed the real thing.
I know there are so many Indias, but this is one
of mine. It's 1975 and night is falling

on the hill above the bakery, where the hostel
owner—just a girl—leads us into a room
the color of Krishna, the color of Shiva's throat

when he swallowed the poison. There we lay down
our bags. The posters on the wall—a parade
of Krishnas, the fat baby stealing the milk,

him posing on a lotus with his blue rolls of baby fat,
then Radha and her blue boyfriend
wrapped in two versions of the same green sari

so close, so fine you couldn't call them anything
but Radhakrishna (*doo lang doo lang doo lang*)
taped to the ceiling, the way the world's teenage girls

taped the Beatles to their ceilings, till the corners yellowed
and peeled, till the magic faded. We'll sleep there, safe under
Krishna's gaze, so peaceful in God's blue belly.

All Flesh is Blades

Everyone wears black at the beauty school
though nobody's in mourning, except maybe
the little tufts of hacked-off hair
that cower around our feet.

Haircuts are more fun if you grow it long
then get it chopped off all at once,
and the black-haired girl snipping
my curls agrees—I like her

because she keeps stopping
with half my hair uncut to say, *Let's leave you
like this*, and I play along, *Gorgeous, gorgeous*,
until in the mirror, light catches
the row of thin white lines
that ribs her forearms, all parallel,
the way a child illustrates grass.

And though all flesh is blades
of grass, I can't help wondering
how many years she waited for puckered skin
to smooth into pink ridges, how long

it must have taken her
to push up her sleeves,
wash her hands, and take up
the blank-eyed mannequin head
that stares at me from her glass table.

Shorter is fine, I tell her,
and she says, *That's brave of you*,
as she slides the cold scissor blades
closer to my neck.

Game Deaths

The body stiffens, cross-eyed
as it falls. The body splits and wilts,
unfolding its origami shape.
The body drops to the tune
of low chords, to the tune
of "Do Not Destroy." The body
is a ship unmanned, demolished.
The body is a city scraped ragged
by tornadoes' long fingernails.
The glory departed. The body
makes no sound. It is a spaceship
splintered into the dark blue galaxy.
Its eyes are little thumbprints,
little shells. It is a city with no coins.
The body does not believe
in the life of the world to come,
because the body has no beliefs.
It believes in falling.
It believes in jumping.

To an Old Calendar of Paintings of the Blessed Virgin

Mussoorie, India

Lying on the bed below you,
I never managed to ask you to pray
for us, or to see you weep the blood
you're famous for. I just loved to stare—

and you didn't seem to mind—
at your barely blushing cheekbones, lit
by the angel's glow. You warmed me
with your incandescent eyelids

and the light—keen as sunburn—
that sears you as you turn away your face
with a whisper that is always *yes*.
I miss your smile in this place

where grinning Hanumans and resplendent
Ganeshas peer out from every corner.
Their half-human eyes unnerve me.
Where are you now, in some dusty box,

your twelve images growing daily more obsolete?
Where are your faint halos gathering dust,
as my car careens past a truckbed
heaped with lions and goddesses?

I miss you, in a country wealthy with deity, miss
the comfort of a saint, of knowing that even
under centuries of immaculate
makeup, you were history, flesh, and blood.

New Year's Eve, Kochi, 2004

Just days after the tsunami, we traced
the sandy crust of the water level
with our fingers. The square was empty

but all the lights were on. We had nothing
to do but feast on chili garlic prawns
and secret beer from a white teapot. I kissed

your mouth at midnight, and we toasted teacups
with the Sikh-bearded Swedish deejay, his two girlfriends,
and the rock drummer from Liverpool

who swore the ashram showed him how to change.
I found the prawn's sweet body taut
as a grape between my teeth.

Fruit of the sea. I wanted you
to take off my clothes until I became
a heap of laundry. In the basilica,

the Virgin bore up the weight of marigold
garlands, and the incense smoke smelled like
the mosquito coil we burned each night,

sweet cloud of poison, hanging above our bed.
Every time you go back there is less romance.
This is what Vasco da Gama knew,

which is why he tried to leave his bones
on this skinny peninsula which was in fact
the end of the world, fortressed, buttressed,

for no one to admire, except the Virgin,
who also wished to remember Portugal
the way she left it, a glittery crust of sand.

Landscape with Acacia Tree

Maasai Mara, Kenya

Three-quarters of the picture is all sky,
a dull cerulean mottled with light
in the top righthand corner. That was a cloud, maybe.
And that thickening of blue

was the Great Rift Valley. Neither of us
was much of a photographer. Look how
the foreground grass blurs, like you shot this
from the safari van, the van whose door

rattled ajar to let your sandal slip
into the savanna, while you sat
cross-legged, shoeless, absorbed in *Fear
and Trembling*, trying to forget how tired

we were of grass, zebras, and wildebeest.
Let's say you looked up from your book,
found yourself on this tawny plain.
Your eyes met the tree that twists on the edge

of the photograph like it's trying to escape.
Then what? I can see this much,
but the past grows blurry like blades of grass,
like our attempts at philosophy. Two weeks later,

planes would crash into the world,
their contrails lining an exit path
in the sky. I guess you wanted
to catch something.

You missed. We didn't even know your sandal
had left you already, tossed itself in a dusty rut,
a loss to some Maasai shepherd who'd find it,
days later, no match for his left foot.

Rush Hour Apocalypse

"In case of rapture, this car will be unmanned."
—bumper sticker

In case of rapture, let our engines die,
let their grease-soaked spirits funnel up
to cruise around the sweet by-and-by.

In case of rapture let the earth embrace
the freeway in its viny arms; let every tunnel
be exalted, every overpass made low;

let the viaduct lie down with the sea.
This I prophesy—because once, in a case
of rapture at sunlight through trees

and the moment's photographic possibilities,
I drove this car into a mailbox perched too close
to the road and had to pay the owner

fifty bucks. It's true. So I say unto you
pre-trib sky-gazing schmucks,
keep your eyes on the goddamn road. For behold—

look into oncoming traffic and see we are already
a river of souls coursing over the hill; our lights
flow through the dawn like offerings in the arms

of Mother Ganga—each lamp a candle
that bobs downriver in a leaf-boat toward
the gathering hymn—*O sinner, come home.*

The Virgin in the City

If she were out of work, she'd ride the bus
all day, just knitting, sitting in the dark
knuckle between bus halves, lulled by accordion
folds. She likes the smell of worn-out men—
stale smoke, damp boots, and salt—it makes her feel
useful, wanted. Her work is walking library stacks,
and where her fingers trail frayed spines,
worn threads reweave themselves.
Under her footprints, marble floors regain
their gleam. She hovers in the reading room,
smelling the sour breath of strangers, for
whatever she smells turns holy in her nose.
She sounds out syllables with jittery students,
turns pages for the tired, and when they nod,
she blesses their exhausted sleep. Outdoors,
she opens empty freight containers, carries
wood to trash-can fires, draws water
from the wind and air, and pricks
the snowed-in city's sickened heart, an egg
she broods over, warming it at her breast.
And just before dawn, she alights
in the museum lobby, trips the neon
switch to glow in its warm buzz of sin.
The angel is waiting. The child has slept
but must be fed. So, trailing her shawl behind her,
she walks the labyrinth home.

The Rain Falls on the Just and the Unjust

on the stylish yellow rainboots and the soggy sneakers
on the perennial beds and the shock of volunteer petunias
on the brown leaves and the green leaves
on the rat-faced starling and the ivory-billed woodpecker
     which may or may not exist
on the hard crust of sand at the top of the beach
     and the barnacles sucking the air at low tide
on the place we made love in the woods and the place right next to it
     where we did not make love
on the skinny girls and on the fat girls
on the boys with accents and the boys who stutter
on the catalogues and the phone books, lists within lists on
     cheap paper that wrinkles because it is raining
on the T-shirt with the cutoff sleeves and on the sleeves
on the pizza box and on the revolving restaurant
on the tomb of the unknown soldier and the known soldier
on the shriveled brown stalks of the flood-damaged corn
     adding insult to injury and on the flooded parking lots
on America because that is where I live and can tell you about it
on the public fountain and on the puddle from the public fountain
     because it is improperly drained
on the sidewalk and the drowned earthworm
     and the gutter clogged with leaves
on the city where everyone tells you it always rains and on the city
     where it never rains, ever, except for right now
on the dying, spawning salmon, who have seen every kind of water
     and on the eggs, who have not seen anything yet

Sight Singing

New to the hymnal,
I fumbled forward, note by note, unsure
which stone in the river

to step on next. The water rumbled with centuries
of voices, and under
the book, our fingers touched, sparking

a descant that flowed out
into next year. When the priest called, *Lift up
your hearts*, she sounded

like hers was held already in God's hand.
And when I heard
the gravel rasp in your throat, a little flat,

even though one bass
note swelled behind me, and a tenor to the right
shifted his weight,

it was your scrape of rocks on riverbed
that ferried me
downstream, that carried me into the land.

To the Gleaners

You do not need me to bless you
for the shorn field easily gives up its treasure
into your baskets. Your quick fingers
conjure food out of early-morning mist,
and in this light even the dumpster
gives up its chipped vase, its clawfoot end table.
The sidewalk gives up its clear brown bottle.
You do not need me to bless you,
but I will wish you clear sight
into the world's crevices and corners.
Harvest the chives flowering under the workbench.
Harvest the copper tubing looped in the scrap pile,
the chrome-fendered bicycle at the sidewalk sale.
Clamp the broken slats of the chair together.
Restring the guitar. Let your metal detectors
whine always with joy. May you find all you seek,
because at the end of the story
the woman knots up her apron
heavy with grain, then steals up to the sleeping body
of the man who does not yet love her.
And when she lies down beside him
she will gather even the scent of his sleep—
the smell of her future harvests, ripening.

Single-Point Perspective

Jama Masjid, Delhi, India

I walk along a marble line that gleams
like the perspective lines stretching away
toward the vanishing point we traced

and then erased in art class, smeared mistakes
that wouldn't converge, that even with a ruler
never came out this plainly pure. Look how

rows of red-edged arches open mouths
to call *Allahu akbar*. Shah Jahan,
everyone loves your tomb, the Taj Mahal,

but in your Friday mosque, I become
a point in faith's geometry. My eyes
move along lines to that vanishing point

where they converge—outside, maybe,
in the car parts bazaar or a chai stall.
Somewhere beyond it lines open, all pointing

to other things—Red Fort, the Himalayas,
one woman on her face toward Mecca,
her praying body open as her mouth.

The Witch Sings a Bach Chorale

Europe held the first lover
I ever conjured. It was raining;
it was a century when architecture
diminished all lovers to ghosts;

it was a cathedral loft; he was a boy
who'd learned his counterpoint.
He braided a chorale into my hair
all down my spine, vertebra

by vertebra, *Wachet auf*—
and in the fugue that followed,
I saw the organ pipes transformed
from skinny fingers begging heaven's favor

into a breathing country that bloomed
like coral outward from the deep
vibrating basin where he worked,
where stained glass lit his skin.

For his pale continent, I charmed
the stones to throb like chords,
enchanted my own throat
to split and weave four holy notes.

And though for years I'd walk his labyrinth,
hardly aware the thread I clutched
was braided from four strands,
and though, after it all, he blinked

bewildered at me and returned
to his blank altar, I kept the tenor line
vibrating in his ear, knowing neither of us
could ever lose faith in song.

The Multitude

For you are not alone. For even as you walk alone
down your empty street, their breath presses on you,
dank and close in the late summer air. For though the dead
wait patiently at the back of your neck, their number
grows daily; gray figures line up under the placards
War and Genocide and Cancer, and crowding closest to you

are the incongruous dead you claim only slightly:
the great-grandfather with his head cracked open on the ice,
the opera singer in her crumpled plane, the Air Force pilot
in his crumpled Volkswagen, the professor and the kindergarten girl
clutching twin brain aneurysms, the flautist and scientist and art student
slumped in their still-running cars. You could do nothing for them—

for the future dead, the murmuring populations
of the heart, rise up waiting to be fed—parents, children,
and grandparents of course, but also in-laws, cousins,
the string of people about whom you've fantasized,
the poor you were supposed to have been serving
years ago in another country, and all your lost

and distant friends, huddled at desks in other states,
tossing insomniac all night, panicking over the bills, trying
drugs or speaking in tongues, falling into and out of marriages
you have no power to arrange or even assuage. You pray
for peace, pray they will go away and leave you in peace,
but they won't. Listen, if Christ arrives to feed the multitude

inside you, it won't be the kind of miracle you expect.
He'll bring them a tray of stale biscuits and too-sweet tea,
a few bananas, hardly enough (you think) to keep them full.
Still, some of them may take and eat. Still, some
may gnaw the biscuits long enough to leave you a little silence, the kind
that makes you wonder what you were meant to hear.

Notes

"Philippians"

> The Tea Fire of November 13, 2008, destroyed hundreds of homes in Santa Barbara, California, including eight buildings and fifteen faculty homes on the campus of Westmont College.

> The theological term *kenosis*, usually referring to Christ's "self-emptying" of divine attributes in becoming human, comes from the Greek word *ekenosen* as it is used in Philippians 2:7.

"In the City of Arias"

> In memory of my former classmate Georgina Joshi (1981–2006).

"St. Augustine Enters the World's Largest Pac-Man Maze"

> The 2011 Lecture "Augustine's Journey" by classics professor Owen Ewald served as inspiration for this poem.

"To the Girl Playing Mario Kart in the Botticelli Room"

> Shigeru Miyamoto is the Nintendo game designer who created Mario, Zelda, and Nintendo Wii, among many other popular characters, games, and gaming platforms. In his work *Super Mario Clouds* (2002) artist Cory Arcangel hacked Super Mario Brothers so that all of the graphics were removed except for the clouds, which move across the screen.

"To the Ghost Who Put His Arm Around Me at the Camp Meeting"

> In Cane Ridge, Kentucky, an enormous camp meeting revival drew between 10,000 and 25,000 people during the first week of August, 1801. An anxious bench is a seat near the revival preacher's pulpit where people worried about their souls could come to receive prayer.

"Your Own Calcutta"

> The headquarters of Mother Teresa's order, the Missionaries of Charity, is located on A.J.C. Bose Road.

"Ghost House Level"

Ghost houses first appeared in Nintendo's Mario games in *Super Mario World*, released in 1990. The first two and final lines of this poem were taken from a Facebook post by artist Kevin Buist.

"To the Church Across the Bridge Who is Claiming the City for God"

"The gulf between Man and God" is a phrase taken from *The Four Spiritual Laws*, a religious tract by Bill Bright, founder of Campus Crusade for Christ.

"Meditation on the Divine Blueness with Two Pop Songs"

Bright Tunes Music Corp. successfully sued George Harrison for copyright infringement, based on the similarities between the Chiffons' song "He's So Fine" and his "My Sweet Lord." The case was finally decided in 1976.

"Game Deaths"

This poem was inspired by the video of the same name, created by Rob Beschizza and posted at *Boing Boing*.

"The Witch Sings a Bach Chorale"

Wachet auf, ruft uns die Stimme, (Sleepers, wake…) is the title of a Bach chorale cantata (BWV 140) based on a Lutheran chorale of the same title.

Acknowledgments

Thanks to the editors of journals in which the following poems first appeared, sometimes in earlier versions:

Books & Culture: "The Virgin in the City"

Crab Orchard Review: "Haight Street, Halloween," "In the City of Arias," "Landscape with Acacia Tree" & "Pallas Athena"

The Christian Century: "To the Gleaners"

Christianity and Literature: "Philippians"

Exit 7: "Game Deaths," "On the Drill Field at Virginia Tech," "The Rain Falls on the Just and the Unjust" & "Your Own Calcutta"

Image: "A Natural History" & "To an Old Calendar of Paintings of the Blessed Virgin"

Floating Bridge Review: "Anatevka, Indiana," "Meditation on the Divine Blueness with Two Pop Songs" & "To the Ghost Who Put His Arm Around Me at the Camp Meeting"

The Hampden-Sydney Poetry Review: "Burlington Northern Apocalypse," "To the Body Carried Out of the Apartment Across the Street" & "To the Church Across the Bridge Who is Claiming the City for God"

Los Angeles Review: "The Witch and the Soldier"

The Mennonite: "Sight Singing"

Mid-American Review: "The Multitude"

Rattle: "To the Former Self in Art Class"

Relief: "Single-Point Perspective" & "The Disaster Tourist"

Rock and Sling: "New Year's Eve, Kochi, 2004" & "Rush Hour Apocalypse"

Slate: "A Guide for Spiritual Tourists"

So to Speak: "All Flesh is Blades" & "The Witch and the Scientist"

Southern Indiana Review: "Endor (Disambiguation)"

Spirituality and Health: "Compliment"

Several of these poems are included in a chapbook, *Ghost House* (Floating Bridge Press, 2013).

I am surrounded by an incredible network of friends and writers, many of whom have taken an interest in my work and offered their thoughts on this manuscript. Special thanks to readers Laura Bramon, Jenny Burdge-Patel, Susanna Childress, Kelly Davio, Ben Debus, B.H. Fairchild, Hannah Haag, Kyle Heys, Chris Hoke, Rebecca Jordan Heys, Sarah Kraybill Burkhalter, Roberta Kwok, Marilyn Chandler McEntyre, Kathleen Norris, Amanda Marie Sparkman, Ryan Teitman, Brianna Van Dyke, and Jessie Van Eerden. Thanks to Gala Bent for the beautiful art and inspiring conversations. And deep gratitude to Anne M. Doe Overstreet, Marjorie Manwaring, Arlene Kim, and Nicole Hardy for writing and reading together and for being supportive, creative, smart, and lovely. I'm also indebted to friends and coworkers at Seattle Pacific University and to the support of Indiana University and the Milton Center.

Thanks to Michael Waters for selecting this manuscript, and thanks to Ron Mitchell, Marcus Wicker, and the *Southern Indiana Review* crew for all their work on making this manuscript shapely and beautiful.

Thanks to the Notess and Hiskes families for continuous love and support. And thanks most of all to Jon, Sam, and Theo, who bring me so much joy.

Photo Credit: Luke Rutan

Hannah Faith Notess is the author of *Ghost House*, a chapbook of poems (2013), and *Jesus Girls: True Tales of Growing Up Female and Evangelical* (2009). Her poems have appeared in *Rattle, Slate, Los Angeles Review*, and *Image*, among other journals. She is the managing editor of Seattle Pacific University's *Response* magazine. Learn more about her work at *hannahnotess.com*.

This publication is made possible by the support of the Indiana Arts Commission, the National Endowment for the Arts, the Vanderburgh Community Foundation, the University of Southern Indiana College of Liberal Arts, the USI Foundation, and the USI Society for Arts & Humanities.

The Michael Waters Poetry Prize was established in 2013 to honor Michael's contribution to *Southern Indiana Review* and American arts and letters.

MWPP Winners

2014—Dennis Hinrichsen & Hannah Faith Notess
2013—Doug Ramspeck

Southern Indiana Review Press